The Charcuterie Boards Bible

365 days of Inspiring and Great-Tasting Boards to Celebrate Your Special Moments | Simple Ideas to Impress your Guests

By
AMBROSE BAXTER

© **Copyright 2023 by** AMBROSE BAXTER **All rights reserved.**

This document is geared towards providing exact and reliable information in regard to the chapter and issue covered. The publication is sold with the idea that the publisher is not required to render accounting, officially permitted, or otherwise qualified services. If advice is necessary, legal, or professional, a practiced individual in the profession should be ordered.

- From a Declaration of Principles which was accepted and approved equally by a Committee of the American Bar Association and a Committee of Publishers and Associations.

In no way is it legal to reproduce, duplicate, or transmit any part of this document in either electronic means or printed format. Recording of this publication is strictly prohibited, and any storage of this document is not allowed unless with written permission from the publisher. All rights reserved.

The information provided herein is stated to be truthful and consistent, in that any liability, in terms of inattention or otherwise, by any usage or abuse of any policies, processes, or directions contained within is the solitary and utter responsibility of the recipient reader. Under no circumstances will any legal responsibility or blame be held against the publisher for any reparation, damages, or monetary loss due to the information herein, either directly or indirectly.

Respective authors own all copyrights not held by the publisher.

The information herein is solely offered for informational purposes and is universal. The presentation of the information is without a contract or any guaranteed assurance.

The trademarks that are used are without any consent, and the publication of the trademark is without permission or backing by the trademark owner. All trademarks and brands within this book are for clarifying purposes only and are owned by the owners themselves, not affiliated with this document.

Table of Contents

Introduction **8**

Chapter 1: Building Curated Boards **11**

1.1 Boards *14*

1.2 Stocking *16*

1.3 Setting aside *17*

1.4 Scheduling *18*

Chapter 2: What to Put? **19**

2.1 Sections of a Charcuterie Board *20*

2.2 Charcuterie cheeses *23*

2.3 Best condiments *23*

2.4 Best Crackers and Bread *24*

2.5 Best Fruits, Pickles, and Nuts *25*

2.6 Charcuterie board drinks *26*

Chapter 3: Making a Charcuterie Board **27**

3.1 Choose a Board and Utensils *28*

3.2 Cheese First *30*

3.3 Stack, Slice, and Fold the Meat *31*

3.4 Add Sweets *32*

3.5 Pickles and Sauces *32*

3.6 Bread and Crackers *33*

3.7 Cheese with Fruits and Vegetables *34*

3.8 Fill the Remaining Spaces *34*

3.9 Serve the drinks *35*

3.10 Know your Guest *35*

3.11 Quantity and Quality *36*

3.12 Be health conscious *37*

Chapter 4: Charcuterie's Three Elements 38
4.1 Flavors *38*

4.2 Textures *40*

4.3 Colors *41*

4.4 Tips and Tricks *41*

Chapter 5: Boards Preparation For Home 44
5.1 Fig, Ham, Spinach Board *45*

5.2 Chocolate and Nuts Board *47*

5.3 Cheese, Meats, and Fruit Board *49*

5.4 Cheese Board *51*

5.5 Summer Blossom Board *53*

5.6 Spanish Classic Board *55*

5.7 Antipasto Board *56*

5.8 Straightforward Charcuterie Board *57*

5.9 Charcuterie Flatbreads Board *58*

5.10 Fall Charcuterie Board *60*

Chapter 6: Special Boards For Picnics 62
6.1 Sweet Potato Board *64*

6.2 Pancake and Frittata Board *66*

6.3 Loaded Brunch Board *69*

6.4 Southern Charcuterie Board *70*

6.5 Pecan Charcuterie Board *71*

6.6 Fall Charcuterie Board (Birthday edition) *73*

6.7 Cuddle Board *75*

6.8 Keto Charcuterie Board *77*

6.9 Happy Dessert Board.. *79*

6.10 Dinner Charcuterie Board *81*

Chapter 7: Boards For Sports Days..........................**83**

7.1 Patriotic Charcuterie Board *85*

7.2 Hot Dog Charcuterie *87*

7.3 Gluten-Free Charcuterie Board *89*

7.4 Mac and Cheese Charcuterie Board *90*

7.5 Simple Lunch Charcuterie Board............................... *91*

7.6 Deli Sandwich Board.. *92*

7.7 Barbecue Charcuterie Board....................................... *93*

7.8 Mini Individual Charcuterie Board *93*

7.9 Plant-Based Charcuterie Board.................................. *95*

7.10 Valentine's Day Charcuterie Board *97*

Chapter 8: Seasonal Charcuterie Boards **99**

8.1 Spring... *99*

8.2 Summer *100*

8.3 Fall *100*

8.4 Winter... *100*

8.5 Regional Charcuterie *101*

8.6 Tips For Arranging a Charcuterie Board *102*

Chapter 9: Charcuterie Trends **105**

9.1 Vegan Charcuterie Board.. *105*

9.2 Charcuterie Cones *106*

9.3 Jarcuterie.. *106*

9.4 Dessert Charcuterie... *106*

9.5 Charcuterie Skewers *107*

Conclusion 109

Most used ingredients 111

Introduction

One of the best concepts in the long and illustrious history of dining and hosting parties is the serving of food on sharing boards. Beyond the scope of a standard meal served on a plate, it is a sign of hospitality and admiration for the culinary arts. More individuals are brought together via sharing, eating, and connecting during a board game night than at a regular meal served at a table. And not only are boards enjoyable to eat, but they're also entertaining to make and look at. In most cases, the appetizer, main dish, or dessert at a party will all be served on a board, and this will make it the focal point of the event. People are drawn to it like a magnet and congregate around it, cooing and aahing over it as if it were a newborn as they stuff their faces with all the delicious things it has to offer. In most cases, has something for everyone, or at the very least, there is the potential for there to be. Because they include a range of different dishes, boards are perfect for sharing with a group of people.

They provide everyone, particularly children, the opportunity to try new foods since they give people the control to pick what they eat and design their plates and meals, which makes people feel more confident about trying new things. When presented with a delicious board, even the most finicky eaters are more likely to give something unfamiliar a go and discover that they genuinely like it. The fact that putting such a board for any event requires very little work is one of the many advantages of having this capability. In just a few short minutes, you can fashion a lovely board out of the materials you already have on hand. It's a mindset that involves being aware of what you already have and what you could need in the future. You most likely already own several products that would work well on your board. This allows you to make excellent use of pantry basics as well as anything that you could have in your refrigerator or freezer. Reusing food in new ways, cleaning out the refrigerator, and feeding guests without having to cook may all be achieved with the help of boards.

Any food or meal you like may be brought on board! Building a board that is tailored to the event that you are hosting, whether it be a dinner party, a football watch party, a birthday party, a baby shower, an engagement ceremony, or even simply a children's film night, is very rewarding and is certain to amaze your guests.

When it comes to constructing a board, you can make it as laid-back or as elegant as you desire. You may use the speedy method of heaping everything on and filling up every free place, or you can take your time to create a festive and aesthetically pleasing masterpiece. It's all about becoming creative with the food you make and presenting it in a manner that's interesting and appealing to the customer. Because we eat with our eyes first, something as easy as shaping your children's snacks into a charming shape or overloading a board with a magnificent array of meats and cheeses may provide for a memorable dining experience that you will want to reproduce again and again.

The objective is to be able to prepare the board ahead so that you can also share the thrill with your family members and have very little maintenance to perform while the event as well as very few dishes to clean up later. The creation of an effective board does need some planning, but once you have an understanding of the idea, you will find yourself returning to it time and time again as a mealtime and entertainment choice.

There's a reason why charcuterie boards are all the rage right now: they're delicious.

Who doesn't like a tasty snack? Simply scrolling through Instagram or Pinterest will almost certainly lead you to come upon one. Meats, bread, mushrooms, fruit, and crackers are the components that make up a traditional charcuterie board. Figuring out how much sausage and cheese to purchase might be a bit of a challenge at times. By giving you a brief description of the percentages that each of these components should make up, I want to make the process of building your snack board a bit less difficult for you. What do you know, It couldn't be simpler!

Chapter 1: Building Curated Boards

When using practically any board, the first step that should be taken into account in order to achieve a sense of equilibrium throughout the board is to position any serving dishes there. After that, arrange the other components in the order of their size, starting with the biggest. If there are any products on the board that must be served at a warm temperature, you should make preparations to place them on the board last. Apples and pears that have been cut should be added to the board very last since they tend to turn brown very rapidly. If you want to keep your sliced apples and bananas fresh until you're ready to serve them, you can either cover them with a moist paper towel or sprinkle them with lime juice. Arrange the components so that they are adjacent to one another on the board if they are complementary to one another or go very well together. The beauty and appeal of the board are heightened by the addition of a few simple details, such as spreading out the chips around the bowls and top, sprinkling the hummus with oils, and adding some fresh herbs that complement the dishes. It is best to store items that are prone to become soggy, such as crackers and almonds, in separate areas from those that contain a lot of moisture, such as freshly cut citrus and roasted vegetables that have been rinsed and patted dry. During the winter holiday season, it is customary to provide a charcuterie board. The essentials are straightforward, regardless of whether you want to provide your board to your loved ones as an appetizer or to create a replica of it that you may use for a private online get-together. The selection of a great mix of meats, cheeses, vegetables or antipasto, nuts, spreads, and crisps, is the vital step in producing a well-curated charcuterie board. Any board may be given a more celebratory air with only a handful of thoughtful additions over the holiday season.

First things top, if you want to make a first-rate charcuterie board, you need to respond to the following questions.

- Do you prefer to concentrate on a certain nation or area, or do you wish to combine elements from a variety of nations?
- What variety of food is available to you in the store closest to your home? Do you need the services of a specialized grocery store? Do you plan to place an order for the item if you are unable to locate it locally?
- What kinds of dietary restrictions or individual interests are you required to take into account?

A charcuterie board is not only comprised of the items that are consumed on it but also the presentation of those items and the way they are organized. After you've decided which components to use, the next step is to consider how you'd like to lay up your board. Here are some concepts to consider:

- Arrange everything to be cut on a level wood table, such as countertops or a wide cutting board. If there are any vegans on your guest list, you may want to think about adding more surfaces to separate the meats.
- Color-code numerous platters. The splashes of color come from the garnishes, which may be jam, fruit, or pickles. Arrange them in a neat pattern on the white plates. (You might, for instance, put all of the jams in individual bowls on one dish and all of the fruit on another platter, etc.) Use different colored plates to highlight and contrast the bread, meats, and cheeses on your table.
- Attach a few tags to each product with brief explanations of what they are, where they came from, and any relevant nutritional information that should be included.
- At this point, you are able to begin putting together the various parts of your gourmet charcuterie board.

To begin, let's talk about how much meat you'll need; it's probably going to be less than you anticipate. Because charcuterie is such rich fare, just a little amount goes a very long way. If the charcuterie is served as an appetizer or starting dish, plan on serving each individual around 2 ounces. If somehow the charcuterie is going to be the main course at your event, you should plan on serving each guest around 5 ounces of it. It's a smart move to provide a selection of different kinds of meats to choose from. The two fundamental classifications are known as related materials (raw cured meat) or Cotto (cooked meat). It is a good idea to maintain a balance between the saltiness and intensity of cured meats like prosciutto and the fatty richness and natural flavor of cooked meats such as ham. The food that you put on your board will change according to what you are able to buy and what you choose to put on it. Here are some choices that are both well-known and time-honored.

Gather your Boards and Additives

A well-stocked pantry and refrigerator freezer eventually create boards in a snap. Fruit and vegetables prepackaged munchies, snacks, and some store-bought products contribute to making it fast and easy.

Arrange All Products Upon The Table

Place any serving dishes on the board initially, then the other treats, from greatest to tiniest.

Fill Things Up

A lavish board is appealing and tempting, so please continue to load it up and stuff in all the cracks and crevices with treats that seem to be sure to be loved.

Present Your Work to Friends And Relatives

You really would like to share your lovely and wonderful board creations, obviously.

- Loosen up.

You accomplished all the scheduled work because you can be there with your dear ones as they savor your wonderful masterpiece rather than in the kitchen cooking additional food.

- Love its sweetness

Enjoy the moment with your near and dear ones.

You will be successful no matter how much or how little experience you have in the kitchen. Only one rule applies, and that is you can do whatever you want, Simply be creative, have fun, and most of all, take pleasure in the process, from constructing it to serving it.

Let's just not wait to get our hands on all of the gorgeous and mouthwatering boards that are included in this book, but before we get to that, let's speak about the tricks of the trade. It is common to get confused or shocked by the amount diversity of boards as well as other presenting equipment, which each comes in a variety of sizes and forms. In this book all the straightforward rules to follow are discussed you'll just have to employ them!

1.1 Boards

When you are beginning from scratch and are looking to add some boards to your collection, I have a few recommendations for you.

A very good option is a classic wooden board, but other options include marble, stone, and even slate. There are many various types of board materials available to pick from. Hardwoods are my preference for board materials; therefore acacia, mahogany, ebony, and plum are some of my favorites. You wouldn't want to spend on a board, acacia is an excellent choice for you to consider. If you are only going to have one board, it's good that you choose a big circular hardwood board that is 19 inches or 52 centimeters in diameter. The appearance of a circular board is really appealing to me, and you should search for something that is big enough to seat at least seven people comfortably. The next thing you need to do is get a sizable rectangular board, one which is around 22 inches by 13 inches (52 centimeters by 35 centimeters). A shorter rectangular or circular board that may serve between two and four people would be a good choice for the third addition to your collection of cutting boards. Once you have these three boards, you may start to expand your collection by adding items that have distinct contours, dimensions, and construction materials. But the most important thing is, to remember to treat yourself, and don't stress if your board isn't perfect; after all, it's not about the food or the company, it's about the experience!

You will need a selection of serving bowls or ramekins in conjunction with the board, in order to hold the various dips and condiments. Ramekins and bowls stoneware, glass, as well as other materials, all of which come in a range of sizes and forms, can be used with creativity. Some go-to portions are three ounces for olives and dips, while one ounce is perfect for creams, honey, and sweets. When it comes to preparing, you should also have an assortment of knives, stirrers, and forks at your convenience. When chopping slices or pieces of sharp cheddar, a blade with a spade-shaped blade performs excellently. A knife made especially for smearing soft cheeses, including such as Cheddar, on wafers is referred to as a soft cheese knife. When splitting crumbly foods or slashing and chipping firm cheeses, a dairy knife with a flat blade is the preferred tool. Cheese planes are helpful to have anyway for slicing cheese as you're prepping it or for serving it on the board. It's also good to have a knife for each type of cheese, a spatula for each type of jam or spreading, and a syrup dipper for whenever I need to drizzle honey over things.

1.2 Stocking

When it comes to getting prepared for meals or snacks, having a well-stocked cabinet and refrigerator makes constructing boards a very simple and handy alternative. I try to make sure that I will always have my favorite snacks on hand by purchasing them in large quantities so that I can always have a board ready to go.

The following is a list of the things that I make an effort to always have in stock:

Fruits

Grapes, cherries, raspberries.

Vegetables

Carrots, peas, cabbage, walnuts, cucumbers, pickles.

Cheese

Including cheddar cheese slices, white cheddar that is of high quality, goat cheese, and string cheese are other examples.

Meats

Pepperoni of high quality, chopped turkey, and a salami stick that can be split into thin rounds.

Dressings

Maple syrup, tahini, mayonnaise, nut butter, berry jam, jalapeño, and citrus spreads.

Snacks

Such as crackers, crisps, nachos, almond butter, and corn.

Sweets

Including chocolate-covered walnuts, fresh apricots, yogurt-covered pretzels, and mini biscuits.

Choose meals that can be stored successfully at room temperature while you are putting together your board. The main monopoly of the board is designed to be easy to build yet tedious to play. Because we are talking about nibbling and snacking, you need to be sure that the items you choose can be consumed during the whole dinner or get-together.

1.3 Setting aside

If you want to create your board beforehand, put everything on it that can be refrigerated, then wrap only the head of the board with bubble wrap and put it in the fridge. If you really want to prepare your board in advance, put everything on it that can be reheated. You will need to wait just before dishing the board to add anything that has to be cooked, such as waffles or flatbread rolls, as well as any crunchy treats, such as biscuits and nuts, to protect them from becoming mushy. This will ensure that the crunchy snacks do not get soggy. If you do decide to store a completed or partly finished board in the refrigerator, ensure to take it out an hour before you serve it. This will enable the food, particularly any cheese, to start returning to ambient temperature, which will enhance the taste.

1.4 Scheduling

The length of time needed to construct each board varies as per the degree of difficulty of the design as well as the preparation of the components. Your daily snack board is designed to take around 15 mins to make and uses ingredients that are easy for you to get. Your level of accuracy and speed will determine how long it takes you to complete the seasonal forms. You should not take the boards excessively seriously. This is the single most essential thing you can do. The whole thing is to encourage you to laugh and understand the thrill just as much as the instant you get to share it with the people you care about the most.

With the addition of a stunning and appetizing food board, you can take any event from excellent to amazing in an instant. Each one of the boards has a delightful assortment of treats that are sure to put a smile on everybody's face. Because they are simple and fast to create, they are ideal for any kind of assembly, regardless of their size. All of them are aware that in the event that some people are unable to prepare dinner because they lack either the expertise or the necessary supplies, there will be a delicious board constructed using the food that is already available.

So, go ahead and ask the neighborhood over for a meal of munchies on Sunday evening, or put the children to bed early so that you can appreciate some quiet time with your spouse - a lovely board can be constructed at a moment's notice.

Chapter 2: What to Put?

When preparing a charcuterie, it is essential to have a solid understanding of one of its primary objectives, which is to produce flavor blending by incorporating contrasting tastes into each mouthful. One of the methods to do this is to combine a savory bite with a sweet nibble. This happens because salt brings out the sweetness in other tastes. As a result of this contrast, salty cheeses like brie pair particularly well with grapes.

To round out the range of sensations and tastes presented by the bite-sized snacks, alcoholic beverages such as champagne, beer, and margaritas are often served with charcuterie boards. Always keep in mind that the key is to figure out which bites work well with which others. Therefore, make your cheese board a part of your own personal gastronomic journey, and explore many mouthwatering combinations that you may serve to your guests. Mixing and combining different bite-sized morsels until you discover a decent mixture of bites that work well together is the most important step in creating a successful charcuterie board. Therefore, place an emphasis on flavor, diversity, and texture.

A charcuterie board is comprised of the following five primary elements:

- Meats
- Cheeses
- Spreads as well as Seasonings
- Accents
- Beverages

For almost every event, charcuterie may serve as an excellent starter or even the main course. The following are some of the greatest occasions to put together and present a charcuterie spread:

- Charcuterie boards have such an earthy vibe to them, which makes them an excellent choice for a picnic due to their versatility. When you have picked an ideal location for your picnic, it is simple to divide the components into their own bags and then swiftly place them on a platter.

- Whether you're honoring a proposal, a new house, an anniversary, a new baby, or any other life's wonderful milestones, enjoying special occasions with a charcuterie platter is the ideal way to do it.

- Holiday celebrations: since the holiday periods represent one of the busiest events of the year to indulge in delectable cured cheeses, a charcuterie board is indeed the perfect addition to a get-together to celebrate Christmas or the New Year.

- Charcuterie boards are a great option for a simple but attractive starter to present at dinner parties and other social gatherings. They are versatile enough that you could even use them as the main dish if you were having a less formal dinner party.

- Dates may be romantic in and of themselves, but what could be more romantic than sharing a bottle of wine and some good cuisine with the person you love? If you want to make a romantic evening for you and your significant other, charcuterie boards are a wonderful option of food to provide.

2.1 Sections of a Charcuterie Board

According to the chart, the appropriate width for each segment of a food board is approximately one-fifth (or 20 percent) The following are the primary classifications:

Meats

Including an assortment of raw meat and dry-cured meats is one of my favorite things to do.

Cheeses

The use of both firm and soft varieties of cheese ensures that there is a satisfying option for every customer. It is good to start with a cheddar, but rounding out the taste profile with a spreadable, creamy cheese like brie or goat cheese is a great approach to create variety.

Fillers

This may include anything from nuts to olives to pickles to a sweet spread such as honey or jam. The possibilities are endless. In order to make a balanced board, you should make use of both sweet and savory fillers.

Crunchy snacks and soft bread

I'm a big fan of using a wide range of different textures. Be careful to plan out the tastes of the cheeses and proteins on your board so that they complement one another.

Fruit

Selections should include both fresh and dried types of fruit. Not only do traditional foods like cherries and dried apricots taste well, but they also look quite attractive when arranged on a board.

You can balance the taste by doing the following practices:

- Taste is not repeated between well-balanced courses. When cheese is presented in the form of an hors d'aneuvre, it is not included in the main course meal that is brought to the table. Because of the appetite-suppressing effects of sugary meals, fruit is not often offered as an appetizer. The one exception to this rule is grapefruit, having a tangy flavor that awakens the taste buds in the mouth.

- When the initial course is presented in a pastry crust, serving dessert with such a crust that is also baked would be inappropriate.

- If creamy soup is given as the first dish, then the main meal will not feature creamed veggies.

- When the dish is served, the sauce is brought out only once.

Contrasting Textures

The menu is meant to give a variety of textures, including those that are crunchy and silky, to encourage mastication in diners. Raw foods, like carrots and celery, have a crisp feel, which stands in contrast to the smoothness of cooked meals, such as cheese and soup. Foods with a silky consistency, such as pasta drenched in cream sauce, are balanced by the crunch of salad greens.

Contrasting Temperatures

On this well-rounded menu, you'll find both warm and cold dishes to choose from. Because hot meals increase hunger, a hot item is always provided on a menu. The only way you don't follow this rule is when the temperature is exceptionally high, in which case cold food is less bothersome to the taste.

At a dinner consisting of four courses, the first course is served hot, the second course is served cold, the main course is served hot, and the last course is served cold. In order to ensure that the food is served at the appropriate temperature, warm food is placed on warm plates, while cold food is placed on cool plates. Because porcelain is already a cold material when it is touched, porcelain plates do not need to be cooled. They are then heated in an oven at a low temperature (about 150 to 200 degrees Fahrenheit, or 66 to 93 degrees Celsius) in preparation for a hot course. It is also possible to reheat plates by running them through the process of drying in the dishwasher.

Contrasting Colors

A healthy and well-balanced meal will include a variety of items that are different colors. The main course takes center stage on the table, and the rest of the dishes on the menu are chosen to complement it in terms of flavor, warmth, textural contrast, and color.

Contrasting Seasonings

If the happy hour is unusually lengthy, the taste buds on the palate may get dulled by the hors d'oeuvres; in this situation, it is advised that the ensuing courses have food that is well seasoned.

2.2 Charcuterie cheeses

Charcuterie absolutely needs different cheeses. Mix aged gouda as well as asiago with brie or burrata. Rich blue cheese like Roquefort makes the tastiest boards.

Cheeses include:

- Brie, burrata, feta, mascarpone
- Havarti, Muenster, mozzarella
- Gruyere, Manchego
- Parmesan, Gouda, Cheddar, Romano
- Gorgonzola, Stilton, Dunbarton

2.3 Best condiments

The third element of cheese boards is spread, which may also be referred to as accouterments Spread often consists of spreadable meats and sauces. In most cases, they are used to add an additional layer of creaminess to your morsels as well as to amplify the taste. Adding some bottles or bowls of dips and spreads to your charcuterie board gives it not only a whole different texture but also has the potential to bring about entirely new taste combinations. Honey is a common choice for dipping sauces in the sweet category, while horseradish and mustard are conventional options for savory sauces. Cheese spreads are another delicious component that may be added to a charcuterie board. You may also experiment with something that is not as popular, such as a beef spread that is dried. If you want to include a significant number of baguette slices on your board, you may also want to provide some seasoned pouring oil beside them.

In charcuterie, the following are some examples of spreadable meats and sauces that are often used: terrine

- Pâté
- Rillettes
- Honey with various fruit preserves, seasoned
- Dijon, Tangy, and Stoneground are the three types of mustard.
- Tapenades
- Dips such as hummus and bean

2.4 Best Crackers and Bread

In addition to your spreads and condiments, you are going to want to have some crackers and bread available. Do not select crackers and bread that are rich with strong flavors like cheese and herbs since we do not desire them to compete with the flavors of the cheeses and meats. Therefore, while selecting your bread and crackers, choose only from the following range of options:

- Crackers with a neutral flavoring.
- Crisps made from whole grains and wheat.
- Crackers with fruit and nuts on both sides.
- Crackers with the flavoring of sea salt
- Pretzels
- Raisin pecan rye
- Breadsticks
- Flatbreads
- Baguettes and sourdough are two types of traditional French bread.

2.5 Best Fruits, Pickles, and Nuts

Adding culinary accents like fruits, pickled veggies, and nuts to charcuterie boards is a great way to improve the tastes and add new textures. They also act as a palette cleanser after eating all of those rich and salty delicacies. Because of this, the majority of charcuterie boards include a great deal of these accents. A little bit of sweetness and some beautiful color may be added by using fruit on a charcuterie board. Grapes, orange slices, apple sauce, peaches, figs, strawberries, blackberries, and a wide variety of other fresh fruits all have a place of honor on a charcuterie board. Other fresh fruits may also be used. Dried fruits are another good option. You may want to try dispersing some dried apricots, mangoes, or dates throughout the surface of your board. Providing your guests with the option to have a bread slice and cracker with a sugary topping opens up the possibility of including jam, jelly, or relishes of your choosing. Pickles and olives both have a salty, sour taste that goes well with fatty meats and cheeses. Include some olives and pickled vegetables, such as dill pickles and sweet gherkins, in individual bowls and top on your charcuterie board. You have the option of getting one dish of marinated olives of a variety or getting two or three different varieties individually. For the sake of uniformity, you should check to see whether all of your olives have their pits removed or none of them do. You may also incorporate fresh veggies if you wish, in addition to the preserved vegetables already mentioned, such as spicy pickled peppers. Your charcuterie board will benefit from the addition of some salty nuts. Because of their size, they are ideal for putting off until the very end of the process. After the other components of your charcuterie board have been set, you may search for vacant spaces on the board and fill these voids with little mounds of nuts. You may use almost any kind of nut that you choose, including peanuts, pistachios, almonds, and so on. You could also want to add some pretzels to your charcuterie board so that it has a little bit more variation in addition to the salty flavor it already has.

The following is a list of culinary accents that you may experiment with combining in various ways:

- Grapes
- Strawberries
- Thin slices of apples and pears
- Sticks of celery and carrot are also available.
- Cucumbers
- Walnuts, almonds, pistachios, and caramelized pecans are some examples of nuts.
- Dates and raisins may be used.
- Olives with pickled vegetables
- Rosemary, basil, mint, and oregano are some examples of herbs.

2.6 Charcuterie board drinks

A charcuterie platter needs a drink. Non-alcoholic drinks are appropriate for French food, but I prefer wines and cocktails.

Alcohol choice depends on the cheese and meat in the dish. Meat pairs nicely with comparable, non-overpowering booze. Mild meat pairs best with medium-bodied wines, whereas delicate meat with white or light reds. Salty cheeses complement sweet wines.

- Negroni, Manhattan
- Chenin Blanc, Pinot Grigio, Sauvignon Blanc
- Pinot Noir, Syrah
- Cabernet Franc
- Merlot
- Sparkling water, mineral water and lime, stevia sodas

Chapter 3: Making a Charcuterie Board

When it's time to make a charcuterie board, the arrangement of the morsels is the next most crucial stage. You may have observed that everything, even the silverware that is placed on a charcuterie board, has been given careful consideration. Charcuterie boards may be thought of as your very personal culinary work of art in certain respects. Charcuterie boards should not only be savory and functional but also have a pleasant appearance to the eye. Because of this, it's of equal significance to make certain that the meals are organized in the most user-friendly manner possible so that your guests can enjoy them.

A charcuterie board may very well be the only starter that provides a more remarkable sensory experience than any other option. If you've ever been reading your go-to food blog and come across a stunning picture of a charcuterie board, you've probably been forced to pause for a few seconds to take it all in and let your mouth moisten in response to the sight. The best part is that you do not need to be a culinary mastermind or an artist in order to make a charcuterie board that is both attractive and delectable. Any person is capable of making charcuterie boards that are not only tasty but also attractive by adhering to a few fundamental guiding principles. At your next get-together, whether it be with friends or family, wow everyone with a charcuterie board not only looks amazing but also provides a delectable experience for everyone who partakes in it. This chapter will tell you how you may build such a board.

3.1 Choose a Board and Utensils

The number of guests visiting should guide your decision on the dimensions of the boards. Choose bigger boards or utilize a few different smaller ones if you've got a large group of people to serve. If you like, you could also employ any wooden cutting boards, serving boards, or plates you have available.

I also advise using chopsticks, plates, and butter knives that match one another since they contribute aesthetically to the whole presentation. For the spreads, sauces, and pickled items you will be making, you will also require ramekins and soufflé bowls.

Now next time you go shopping, there are many other possibilities for you to choose from if you do not already possess one of them. You have the option of selecting wood, marble, or slate, in addition to a wide range of sizes and contours. Your goal should be to choose one that can hold all of the many food options you have, but it shouldn't be so big that there are voids in it. It is vital to remember that the quantity of food on your boards should have a direct correlation to the number of guests that you will be feeding. A reasonable rule of thumb is to provide each individual with two pieces of meat and cheese, but if you are entertaining guests who have large appetites, you should alter the amount appropriately. Your charcuterie board needs to be stocked with a selection of mustards, dips, mustard jellies, and preserves. This may include some of my favorite condiments and spreads, such as fig spread, blue raspberry jalapeño pepper jam, parmesan, cashew cream mustard, sour cream, and the list continues on and on. Offer your guests a range of different foods. Bowls are an excellent container for a variety of foods, including fresh mozzarella balls, little almonds, and so on. A variety of dimensions, including sizes, forms, materials, and colors. Now, it should be rather evident that these products need little bowls in order to be confined. However, those bowls have a dual purpose by also performing the function of groundwork for your board. They are solid and strong, making them an excellent choice for leaning crackers against, piling dried fruit beside the, stacking cheese besides, and other similar uses. Put them in various locations around the board. The number, as well as the size, will be determined by the dimensions of your board. A big cutting board, platter, or tray in the shape of a circular or rectangular rectangle to act as the foundation for your charcuterie platter; something simple, such as marble or wood, rather than anything colorful or patterned, so as not to detract from the lovely presentation of the food. Dishes for serving should have a color scheme that works well together and have a range of sizes and heights, such as ramekins, tiny bowls, and medium-sized bowls for condiments like jams, mustards, olives, and almonds, as well as a tall, slender container for breadsticks.

The following are some basic points that can assist you in selecting the appropriate cutlery for the ideal charcuterie board, which should have a variety of tastes, textures, and colors.

- A collection of cheese knives, including those that are particularly sharp for the harder cheeses
- Forks and smaller spoons for spreading jam, mustard, and other condiments, as well as prongs for olives and other fruits
- Toothpicks
- Small plates used for serving

3.2 Cheese First

You should begin by securing your board with cheese, so begin there. Arrange the cheese so that it is slightly offset from the core. To begin, cut your blocks of cheddar cheese into pieces that are suitable for snacking. You can slice them into squares if you want, or triangles or rectangles according to your preference. Keep in mind that you should deal with odd numbers, so choose either three, seven or eight different varieties of cheese. However, when it comes to this course, the unwritten principles of layout may have the biggest impact in the world. Charcuterie boards may give the appearance of lacking structure to the naked eye. It is critical to make sure that cheese and meats are the initial things that are placed on a charcuterie board in order to achieve the desired effect. It gives a map for the taste senses to follow while navigating the plethora of possibilities that are available by arranging the cheeses in a progression from tender to hard and from mild to strong. After the cheeses have been arranged to precision, it is time to go on to the next step, which is adding the meat. Proteins may be arranged in the same manner as cheese, that is, from mild to strong, alongside the cheese flavor that corresponds to that level of intensity. It is good to provide the guest with the appropriate complement for each mouthful of food by combining mild cheese with mild meat.

Traditional charcuterie boards have a significant amount of meat, but it's a good idea to include some cheeses that go well with the different areas or tastes represented by the meats. Think about using a mild cheese like a goat when pairing it with hard and salty salami or use a sharp cheese like cheddar or Swiss when pairing it with pepperoni since it can handle the heat. You might also take into consideration cheeses that are more suitable for the autumn season, such as a Wensleydale cheese that is spiced with cinnamon, ginger, and cinnamon or a cherry goat cheese log.

3.3 Stack, Slice, and Fold the Meat

After that, pile the meat onto your cutting board. After slicing and folding, arrange the pieces so that they fill the gaps between the cheeses. To get the best results, you should fold each one into a half-moon configuration and then spread it out like a cards deck. When dealing with bigger cuts of meat, it is best to split them into quarters and then wrap them up like a scroll.

Experimenting with different ways to fold the meats might help your board achieve an even higher level of visual appeal. You may fold thin foods like prosciutto as well as pepperoni like a string if the meat is on the thinner side. Try wrapping meats that come in curvatures like mortadella and otherwise salami into a rose for more variation. This works especially well with mortadella. Your guests will need cutlery, and you should provide them with little spoons and knives. And since no one enjoys being the one to cut into meats and cheeses initially, you should either chop up a few portions before presenting them or be the one to make the very first cut. Meats that are naturally cured do not include as many artificial preservatives. These meats often get their preservative components from their natural origin such as celery flour or juice as an alternative to the use of nitrates or nitrites that have been artificially added. You should alter your selections according to the requirements of your diet since the exchange is a decreased shelf life as well as a greater level of salt in the food. Consider going for vegetarian choices, even if they go against the basic definition of the meat-based phrase "charcuterie." Vegetarian meat replacements, such as fig salami as well as veggie pepperoni, provide a wonderful taste while having less salt and fat than traditional meat products. This allows you to accommodate the dietary requirements of all of your guests. Instead of cutting the cheeses and meats into cubes, arrange the slices, wedges, and blocks first when arranging them on a platter. Place dishes or containers containing olives, spreads, mustards, and other toppings around the board next to get a sense of the available area. Place fresh fruit, dried fruit, and cheeses that go well together on a platter adjacent to each other. Crackers and bread should be added to the remaining area.

3.4 Add Sweets

Placing spreads and condiments next to the dishes that they enhance is the most effective way to arrange them for presentation purposes. Since the majority of meats and cheeses already have a savory flavor, I suggest beginning with sweeter foods like honey and jams.

In addition to the things that we have previously discussed above, you may additionally include any nuts of your choosing. You may choose to use sauces, spreads, pickled preserves, and herbs in the dish. Be careful not to get any moist foods or sauces on your dry items; if you do, you run the danger of completely destroying the integrity of the taste.

3.5 Pickles and Sauces

After you have arranged the sweet condiments, proceed to add the pickles and savory sauces like Dijon and pesto after you have finished arranging the sweet condiments. Be careful with delicacies such as pickles and olives that need to be placed in ramekins or other tiny bowls in order to prevent other dishes from becoming wet and soggy. Be sure that your charcuterie brings something special to the table when you are creating a dinner that centers on the discussion of flavors. Your charcuterie palate will thank you for embracing a variety of sauces, chutneys, and jams and will grow as a result. Including a delicate sauce, like honey, in the portion designated as mild may have the biggest impact in the world. Don't let the thought of sharp cheddar and spicy meats stress you out since seasoned as well as peppery sauces go well with both of these ingredients. When you pour the dips, jams, and sauces that you've picked into little bowls and then strategically put them on your board, the presentation of your board is much improved. In this manner, everyone will have a few options available to them on their respective portion of the table.

Olives include a high concentration of antioxidants and are a wonderful source of vitamins E, iron, copper, and calcium. However, if you or your guests are watching their sodium intake, you should steer clear of olives that have been preserved in salt water during the packaging process. Also, if you want something sweet, you may want to try adding some dates to your buffet. Although these fresh apricots may have a high-calorie count, they also include a significant amount of fiber (a whopping 7 grams in a serving size of 3.5 ounces!), which may prevent an excessive rise in blood sugar after a meal.

3.6 Bread and Crackers

After that, cut up some of the bread of your choosing and set it down next to the jams. Place your remaining crackers among the various spreads and sauces that you have. On a charcuterie board, bread and biscuits provide the ideal base for guests to enjoy cheese and spreads, and they're sure to come in handy. If you decide to serve bread, use a dense and crusty kind like a baguette from France so that it can be picked up and eaten like other finger foods without falling apart. You might alternatively serve grissini, which is traditionally served to take a stand in a glass. To ensure that you have enough diversity on a bigger board, use at least two distinct types of crackers for the appetizer. Some of them may have a buttery flavor, while others may have a multigrain or nut flavor. Whether you place it on the board or put them on the sides, including a selection of crackers as well as crostini in any charcuterie platter ensures that it will be a smashing success. If the board does not provide enough place for the crackers, don't leave them off the display altogether; rather, create a separate display for them. Autumn confections come in a variety of shapes and sizes, including bite-sized snacks such as toasted chia seeds, salted walnuts, green pepitas (that are similar to pumpkin seeds but lack their shells), walnuts, and even flavored pecans. Snacking on almonds is a healthy choice because they are rich in fiber and nutrition, while plant-based foods are a healthy choice because they are high in vitamin C like vitamin E.

3.7 Cheese with Fruits and Vegetables

Place fruits and vegetables all around cheeses as well as meats on the charcuterie board to create a splash of color. Fruits and vegetables easily have the richest colors of any of the morsels on the board. Vegetables may offer a wonderful splash of color, a satisfying crunch, and a delicious flavor, in addition to providing a number of health advantages. In addition to the conventional options, such as tiny carrots and celery, you may also consider providing fresh asparagus, squash, sugar snap peas, radishes, or a selection of sliced peppers.

3.8 Fill the Remaining Spaces

Last but not least, the empty places on the board should be filled with nuts, including dried fruits and dates. The next step is to garnish your charcuterie board with some stems of herbs, which you may arrange in a circle around the board's center. If you fill the spaces on your board using fresh fruits and vegetables, including grapes, bananas, and a variety of strawberries, not only will your board seem fuller and more professionally created, but it will also provide a reviving complement to the more decadent parts of your board. Fresh vegetables like carrots, celery, tomatoes, and chilies are also wonderful accompaniments, and this is particularly true if your board also includes chutney and dips. When you look at your board, you may be wondering what the finishing touches are that will make it come to life. As we go on to the last stage, we are approaching the point at which the salty and sweet components will be combined. Spreading an even distribution of fresh, dried, and nuts fruits over your board is an excellent way to fill up any holes or spaces that may be present. Grapes are a classic. Can't think of anything more to add, can you? Consider the event that is taking place! If it's the holiday season, stick to seasonal foods like figs, whether they're fresh or dried. Consider the items that you like including if you are unsure of what to provide. Since this board is a representation of your preferences and your own original design, you may as well make it a reflection of who you are as a person.

3.9 Serve the drinks

Pour some red wine or bubbly on the side when you're ready to entertain your guests. You may even offer both. If you don't have any of them, a reviving lime soda or fizzy water would be the ideal beverage to go with your charcuterie board.

3.10 Know your Guest

While putting up a charcuterie board, it may seem like stating the obvious, but it is essential to take into account the number of people you will be serving when purchasing the necessary components. When it comes to this, having a good familiarity with your guests comes in helpful. Do they tend to eat a lot when they become hungry? Is cheese anything that genuinely interests them? Do they have preferences that are more conventional, or do they like trying new flavors? Having this knowledge affects both the kinds of products and the amounts that you purchase. Calculating amounts can be difficult; some sources recommend serving a specific amount of cheese and meat to each guest, but I believe that you should gauge this based on a variety of factors, including the size of the items you are serving, the appetites of your guests, and how much your board will be served as an appetizer or a main course. Naturally, it is definitely preferable to consume too much rather than too little (this is particularly true if your table is the main meal), since you can always keep stuff and then refill them when they run out.

Making yourself a charcuterie board is a lot simpler than you may believe, despite the fact that at first, it could appear challenging. The nicest thing is how simple it can be tailored to your own preferences to fit your needs. If you're going to create something at home, you may as well get the whole gang together and play with it to see who can build the finest charcuterie board.

3.11 Quantity and Quality

Whether your charcuterie board is the biggest feature or is used for snacking, you should place emphasis on quantity and quality in all of your boards, regardless of how large or tiny they are. If the charcuterie board has to be grazed on before a more substantial dinner, it typically comprises three to four slices of meat and three to two ounces of cheese for each person. Make sure that the information regarding who you are serving, as well as any individuals that joined at the last minute, is totaled up before you go shopping for the large stuff. Now that the number has been determined, it is time to think about the excellence of each individual item. Prosciutto and pate are excellent places to begin if you do not have a firm grasp on the types of meats that should be purchased. Choose things that come in a variety of forms, colors, and dimensions so that you and your guests can tell each thing apart.

3.12 Be health conscious

In the event that you or any of your guests have preexisting health conditions such as cardiovascular disease, diabetes, or elevated blood pressure, you need to be mindful of the salt and fat content of your board in addition to the calorie count of the food on it. For a healthy choice, make sure that you include at least one serving of vegetables and fruit for every serving of beef on your board.

Keep in mind that putting up a charcuterie board is not quite an exact science as you do so. Instead, it's more like working on an art piece, and the only way for your boards to improve is via consistent practice and exploration. As you continue to create new delectables for your guests, you should constantly keep in mind methods in which you may add extra taste appropriate to the season as well as a lot of health advantages.

Chapter 4: Charcuterie's Three Elements

The ease with which one may assemble a charcuterie board is one of the primary reasons for the dish's widespread popularity. Either you may create it in advance so that it is ready when your guests begin to arrive, or you can create it to appear after dinner as if by some type of culinary Houdini. Both options are available to you.

The charcuterie board originally served as a meal for peasants and hunters in its most basic form. A piece of hard cheese and a dry-cured sausage, such as a landjaeger, were convenient items to have on hand since they did not need refrigeration and could be quickly transformed into a meal with the addition of a piece of bread and one of their many folding knives. With the aid of these three components, you will be able to transform the ordinary meat and cheese plate into a work of beauty that will wow your guests and excite your taste senses.

Let's go through the 3 components of the charcuterie board that you need to pay attention to while putting it together. It is creative that you ensure a good balance between the many tastes, sensations, and hues in the dish.

4.1 Flavors

A charcuterie board that is worthy of praise provides a variety of flavors, not only to ensure that there is sufficient on the board to satisfy the preferences of a wide range of individuals but also to ensure that each bite provides the individual who consumes the entire platter with a novel experience. Let's begin with the fundamental tastes: salty, salty, and sweet. Obviously, the more space you have on your plate, the more flavors you'll be able to highlight.

Creating a flavor profile that is pleasing to the palate requires a combination of scientific knowledge, trained intuition, and practical experience. An introduction to striking a balance between the five essential flavors in your cuisine is presented here. Umami, sweet, salty, sour, and bitter tastes, together with umami, are the five components that make up our total experience of flavor. The eating experience is elevated to a whole new level when every component is precisely balanced, not just on the plate but also for the entirety of the meal. Understanding the process as both a science as well art is necessary in order to achieve a perfect flavor balance. It's not hard to locate anything salty. There is a good chance that all of the meats you pick have been cured with salt, but the degree to which each of them retains a salty flavor will vary. Adding cured meats such as salami, land jaeger, pepperoni, or bresaola; cheese such as parmesan cheese, Manchego, and asiago; as well as some sundried tomatoes, almonds, or crackers are some ways to add salty tastes to your charcuterie board.

It's true that the category of savory covers a lot of ground. We utilize it to encompass a wide range of flavors, ranging from earthy to tangy to smokey. Therefore, even among your options for savory foods, you should strive to locate diversity. Beginning with earthiness, this quality may be discovered in a wide variety of cheeses, ranging from French cheese to Swiss cheese, in addition to nuts, fruits, or condiments. A dry-cured salami, such as a Cervelat or perhaps an Italian Wine Salami, is my go-to choice when I want a savory tang, while an applewood smoked cheese or a Hungarian Salami is what I go for when I want smoky flavors.

Some people are taken aback when they see sweet foods, such as berries, caramelized nuts, toffees, and jams, on a charcuterie board; nevertheless, these sweets serve more than one function. You can't go wrong with figs encased in prosciutto or a strong cheddar with quince jam; and finally, a few distributed sweets around the plate are like lost secrets to the guests who have a sweet tooth, even vegans and vegetarians.

Spice and acidity are two other flavors to keep in mind if you want to truly take your board to the next level. You don't need a lot of heat, but those who want dishes with a little more kick may get it from pepper salami or Monterey Jack cheese infused with jalapenos. Consider offering them red chili jelly instead, which will ensure that every bite is fiery. Peppers relishes, and mustards provide diners the ability to choose the level of acidity in their meals. Consider providing some, especially if you also plan to serve meats or cheeses with a higher fat or dairy content.

4.2 Textures

In the same way that you want to create a balance between the tastes, you would like to find the right balance between the textures of crunchy and creamy, and hard and smooth. Crackers, nuts, or cornichons might be included as part of your dish's crunchy ingredients. Creaminess may be achieved by consuming a paté de foie, somewhat hard salamis with such a fatty mouthfeel, or a brie cheese made with twice the amount of cream. Think of some of the tougher meats and cheeses (like pepperoni sticks or pieces of land jaeger), some hard cheeses like something of a Comte or a Tome, and dried fruit, or bits of farmhouse bread if you want a solid bite that offers your gums something to grip onto. You may get a silkier texture by using various pesos and dips, rich and creamy cheeses, or fruits and veggies in your dish.

4.3 Colors

This is unquestionably the least crucial of the three components; however, making sure that you have an equitable color palette not only helps make your charcuterie board appealing to the eye but also provides a general cheat sheet to make absolutely sure that you've got the flavoring to adjust right (balayage and shades of red often seem to be salty, yellow ones and whites introduce some savory earthiness, and the vibrant colors include a pop of sweetness).

Be careful to choose some objects for your board that will stand out or "pop" on the board while you are choosing what to put on it. Bright colors such as red (strawberries, cherries, tomatoes), green (grapefruits, cucumber slices, herb garnish), and other bright colors are recommended. There are many dark meals available, and if you are not cautious, your board will seem uninteresting rather than dazzling if you do not diversify it.

Be wary of clustering an excessive number of hues that are the same in close proximity to one another. In terms of presentation, this will be helpful. The same may be said of the texture. Variety is vital. You want certain surfaces that are glossy and smooth, like dates. You want some craggy, jagged surfaces like the ones shown on the Triscuit crackers in the previous image. Some of them have to have a wet or moist appearance, such as the jams and spreads; others ought to be quite dry, like the walnuts and the almonds.

4.4 Tips and Tricks

Some Tips and Tricks to help you in the mak of a Charcuterie Board

Garnishes

The initial and only guideline about toppings is that they need to be edible, and their appearance must be complementary to the food being served. Fresh fruit, such as green grapes as well as sliced nectarines, fresh herb leaves (softer plants, such as basil or cilantro, are preferred to oregano), or, if you want to go fancy, a few edible blossoms or candied rose petals are all simple garnishes that meet both of these criteria.

Labels

If a homemade charcuterie board is intended for a casual social gathering (or if the board itself is tiny), conversing with your guests about the various varieties of cheeses may easily be included in the agenda for the event. It is a wonderful idea to make small labels available for larger events and boards so that people are aware of the food that they are consuming.

Slicing

Food products and charcuterie are at their most flavorful when they are allowed to come to room temperature before being consumed; this enables the textures to become more pliable. Nonetheless, slicing cheeses and meats while they are at ambient temperature is not recommended since it often results in an unpleasant mess. Before you serve the food, do yourself and your guests a favor and slice the salami and cheeses right out of the refrigerator (while they are still hard). This will make everything go much more smoothly.

Layout and presentation

In order to get the most out of this piece of advice, you'll need to exercise your ingenuity and make sure you try out a variety of approaches. I suggest getting the cured cheeses and meats out of the way first since they are the most important components. After that, place additional big objects (such as crackers or bread) on the board, and then construct the remainder of it around those items. you can display the goods that are on your board. For example, you could try stacking the items, arranging your cured meats, or pre-slicing your cheese. You may want to try serving any components that contain the liquid in ramekins, such as olives marinated in oil, chutneys, or dips. This prevents stains on your board and maintains a high level of professionalism in your presentation! Make sure that you provide your board with the proper tools, such as tongs, cutting spoons, napkins, and so on.

Chapter 5: Boards Preparation For Home

There are many different ways to set up a charcuterie board, but in specific circumstances, particular customs dictate how they should be organized. However, one of the greatest joys of assembling a charcuterie board is in the quickest and loveliest manner imaginable. It can be done by arranging the components of the board as per three criteria: tastes, aesthetics, and the convenience of eating them at the table. The objective of talking about all this is to make sure that each of these three components complements the other two while still abiding by the core idea of charcuterie boards. As a consequence, this cookbook takes the simple method of setting up party-worthy presentations utilizing meats, cheddar, freshly picked and dried berries, raw and grilled veggies, and complementing sauces and wafers. So, in the meantime, working on coming up with concepts while also participating in the various event ideas that were submitted on the board, which included innovative diet suggestions. There really is something appropriate for a range of activities, and you and your family members may be able to coordinate fun things to share jointly.

5.1 Fig, Ham, Spinach Board

Serving: 6

Preparation Time: 10 minutes

Cooking Time: 15 minutes

Nutritional information (Per Serving): Calories: 189, Fats: 5g, Carbohydrates: 27g, Proteins: 8g,

Ingredients:

Dressing:

- 1 tbsp of Dijon mustard
- 1 lemon
- 1/3 tbsp of olive oil
- Salt
- Black pepper

Board:

- shallots, sliced
- 2/3 cup of spinach
- 12 figs
- oz of ham
- 1/3 cup of gorgonzola cheese

Directions:

- To make the dressing, combine the lemon juice and mustard in a medium bowl and whisk until creamy. Season with salt and pepper after gradually incorporating olive oil into the ingredients until it becomes blended.
- Combine shallots and spinach in a separate bowl, then pour dressing over the salad and toss to combine.
- The spinach combination should be spread out on the board, and then figs, ham, and the finishing touches should be added with a cheese called gorgonzola.

5.2 Chocolate and Nuts Board

Serving: 6

Preparation Time: 10 minutes

Cooking Time: 0 minutes

Nutritional information (Per Serving): Calories: 129, Fats: 2g, Carbohydrates: 18g, Proteins: 6g,

Ingredients:

- Dark chocolate
- Milk Choco sauce
- 1 cup of sweet chocolate
- 2/3 cup of nuts
- 1 cup of berries
- peeled bananas
- ½ cup of pound cake
- ½ cup of crushed chocolate cookies, muffins, croissants

Directions:

- Place two separate serving dishes in the middle of the board at a distance of about three to four inches apart. Within each bowl, pour about two cups worth of melted chocolate.

- In the same way, arrange the other contents on the board, both around the chocolate bowls and in between them.

- The board should be served with various little instruments, such as sampling forks, tasting teaspoons, micro spatula, and so on.

5.3 Cheese, Meats, and Fruit Board

Serving: 6

Preparation Time: 10 minutes

Cooking Time: 15 minutes

Nutritional information (Per Serving): Calories: 111, Total Fats: 4g, Carbohydrates: 12g, Proteins: 3g,

Ingredients:

- 8 oz of cream cheese
- 2/3 cup of nuts
- Ranch dip (Readymade)
- Cheddar dip (Readymade)
- Honey for spraying
- Meats (curated)
- fresh fruits
- Dried fruits
- Olives
- Chips

Directions:

- Place all of the cream cheese in a bowl and stir it well until it is completely incorporated. After lining a loaf pan with baking parchment, put the cheese inside the pan. Use a spatula to shape the cheese into the shape of the pan. You can put it in the freezer for at least 4 hours, or until the texture is set.

- Until then, put all of the nuts in the bowl of a processor and whirl it a few times till the nuts are roughly blended. Set down.

- Start by removing cheese from the freezer and put it side down in the middle of the board. Push the nuts on top of the cheese in a precise manner to create a beautiful crust. Afterward, you must clean the board.

- Put the dipping sauces and honey in three different dishes, then place them in three distinct places across the board.
- Place cheddar, sauces, and syrup in the middle of the platter, then put the other items around them.
- The board must be served with multiple sampling tools, such as sugar wands, testing forks, buttered knives, tasting teaspoons, and others.

5.4 Cheese Board

Serving: 6

Preparation Time: 10 minutes

Cooking Time: 0 minutes

Nutritional information (Per Serving): Calories: 145, Total Fats: 12g, Carbohydrates: 42g, Proteins: 12g

Ingredients:

- Cherry
- Rasp jam
- Butter
- 8 oz of cured meats
- baguettes, sliced
- oz of blue cheese
- oz of sharp cheddar
- oz of Gruyere cheese

- 4 red apples
- 4 pears
- 2 oz of dried figs
- Roasted cashews
- Crackers

Directions:

- Place some raspberry jam, cherry, syrup, and butter in single-serve dishes and put them aside.
- The same is to be done with the rest of the components; lay them on a big board.
- Arrange rasp jam, cherry, honey, & butter on the side, and present

5.5 Summer Blossom Board

Serving: 6

Preparation Time: 10 minutes

Cooking Time: 5 minutes

Nutritional information (Per Serving): Calories: 125, Total Fats: 2g, Carbohydrates: 41g, Proteins: 11g,

Ingredients:

- Mini baguettes
- ½-inch of thick olive oil
- ½ tsp of garlic powder
- ½ tsp of paprika
- Salt
- cured meats
- Swiss cheese
- Manchego cheese
- ½ cup of tomatoes
- 1 lb. of green grapes
- cups of apricot
- Chips
- 1 cup of caponata
- 1 cup of olives
- 1 cup of roasted favorite nuts

Directions:

- The baguette slices should be arranged on a baking pan before the oven is preheated to 450 degrees F. Coat with olive oil and brush. After that, season the food with salt, pepper, and garlic powder. Roasted bread must be placed in the oven for 4 minutes, or till it has a brown color.

- In the meanwhile, prepare the other ingredients by spreading them out on a big board. Arrange the cured meats, cheddar, peppers, cherries, peaches, water biscuits, and crisps in an attractive manner.
- Caponata, walnuts, and peanuts each should be placed in their own separate bowl. Place the bowls onto the boards.
- Add the baguette pieces and relax

5.6 Spanish Classic Board

Serving: 6

Preparation Time: 10 minutes

Cooking Time: 0 minutes

Nutritional information (Per Serving): Calories: 102g, Total Fats: 12g, Carbohydrates: 22g, Proteins: 14g,

Ingredients:

- 1 cup of eggplant
- 1 cup of roasted bruschetta
- 1 cup of caper
- 1 cup of olives
- 1 cup of grilled artichoke
- Toasted crostini
- 4 types of cheese
- Dried fruits
- fresh fruits
- Crackers and breadsticks
- Cured meats
- Edible flowers

Directions:

- Caponata, bruschetta, capers berries, walnuts, and artichoke pieces should each be arranged in their own separate serving dish. Put the bowls in a line from across the board.
- Prepare the rest of the ingredients and put them on the board. Cover with edible flowers.

5.7 Antipasto Board

Serving: 6

Preparation Time: 10 minutes

Cooking Time: 0 minutes

Nutritional information (Per Serving): Calories: 102g, Total Fats: 12g, Carbohydrates: 22g, Proteins: 14g,

Ingredients:

- 1 cup of marinated artichoke
- 1 cup of olives
- ½ cup of peppadew
- ½ cup of Marconi almonds
- 8 oz of mozzarella
- 1 tbsp of olive oil
- A pinch of chili
- 1 tbsp of parsley
- 8 oz of Asiago cheese
- 8 oz of provolone cheese
- 8 oz of Parmesan cheese
- Assorted meats
- 1 loaf of focaccia bread

Directions:

- Put the artichoke hearts, olives, chiles, and almonds in separate individual dishes. You need to position the cheese on the board.
- Place cheese balls, olives, red chili powder, & garlic powder in a small bowl with parsley.
- Mix the bowl well and place it on the board as well.
- Arrange the remaining components in a different pattern throughout the board, and then serve.

5.8 Straightforward Charcuterie Board

Serving: 6

Preparation Time: 10 minutes

Cooking Time: 0 minutes

Nutritional information (Per Serving): Calories: 93g, Total Fats: 10g, Carbohydrates: 12g, Proteins: 10g,

Ingredients:

- 1 cup of berry
- 1 cup of salami
- 1 cup of prosciutto
- 1 cup of pecans
- cheese types

Directions:

- Arrange the berry jams on a serving plate, and then place the bowl on the cutting board. Place the ingredients in a bowl in an attractive arrangement on the board, and dish.

5.9 Charcuterie Flatbreads Board

Serving: 6

Preparation Time: 10 minutes

Cooking Time: 0 minutes

Nutritional information (Per Serving): Calories: 34g, Total Fats: 14g, Carbohydrates: 28g, Proteins: 15g,

Ingredients:

- ¼ cup of tapenade
- toasted flatbreads
- 6 oz of meat (Any Kind)
- oz of burrata
- 2 tbsp of crushed almonds
- Red chili flakes
- Honey

Directions:

- Divide the tapenade, and half of it is smeared on one-half of each flatbread before being placed on the board.

- Place cured meat, ½ of the burrata, nuts, red chili powder, and almonds on top of it.

- Honey should be drizzled on top. To serve, top the burrata with the leftover tapenade.

5.10 Fall Charcuterie Board

Serving: 6

Preparation Time: 10 minutes

Cooking Time: 0 minutes

Nutritional information (Per Serving): Calories: 44g, Total Fats: 12g, Carbohydrates: 87g, Proteins: 32g,

Ingredients:

- ¾ cup of ricotta cheese
- ¾ cup of jam
- ½ cup of green olives
- ½ cup of almonds
- 6 oz of Manchego cheese
- 9 oz of prosciutto
- 1 cup of Choco pretzels
- 1 ½ cups of assorted crackers

- 6 oz of dried prunes
- 6 oz of salted chocolate
- Butterscotch sweets

Directions:

- Ricotta cheese, jam, plus olives each should be placed in a separate individual dish.
- Arrange bowls on the board, now arrange the rest of the ingredients into similar groups all over the area.
- Present

Chapter 6: Special Boards For Picnics

With the addition of a stunning and appetizing food board, you can take any event from excellent to outstanding in an instant. Each of the following Birthday party boards has a fantastic selection of goodies that are sure to put a smile on everyone's face. Given that they are simple and fast to construct, they are ideal for any kind of event, whatever its size. The loved ones are aware that in the event that the host is unable to prepare dinner because he would lack either the expertise or the necessary supplies, there will be a delicious board constructed using the food that is already accessible. Since a lovely board can be assembled at a minute's notice, you don't need to think carefully about asking your friends over for a meal of appetizers at the birthday party of your beloved one. The next order of business is the most important part of any picnic: the sandwiches. Salmon fans, I have some good news for you: salmon is a popular food that I suggest for a picnic since it goes so well with a variety of other foods. Because the fats in salmon create a rich but balanced flavor when taken with gin, smoky salmon is an unmatched contender for matching with gin. This results in a delightful combination that can only be described as mouthwatering. Include some cucumber on your sandwiches for a sense of refreshing here and there. You may counteract the heaviness of the fish and offer a flavor that is in harmony with the smooth taste of the gin by adding cucumber to the dish.

The smells of gin are enhanced by the addition of cucumber, which also helps to cleanse the palate and makes it easier to appreciate the subtle nuances of the drink. Try these delectable morsels with Basic Gin for a wonderful picnic, and they are a must-have item at all times!

Nuts are always available at bars for a good reason: they are the consummate complement to a diverse range of alcoholic drinks, which is why you can find them everywhere. Not to forget their "grab and go" nature, which makes them a fast and simple appetizer that is perfect for any kind of picnic. With these tasty tiny salty treats, you can't go wrong with any member of our Families of Gins. An absolute must-have for every picnic since it is not only lovely but also so flawlessly gratifying.

Can you conceive of a more perfect combination than gin and chocolate? Indulge your need for something sweet and eat as much chocolate as your heart desires. All types of chocolate, from milk to dark to white, work well separately to create harmony with your preferred kind of gin. The flavor profiles of chocolate pair well with the juniper overtones that are found in our gin, creating a lovely treat that can be enjoyed at any picnic. You may also try strawberries dipped in chocolate; I'm sure you can only imagine how delicious these flavors are. Another option is to try strawberries coated in caramel. Trust us, and these are very important for your picnic.

6.1 Sweet Potato Board

Serving: 6

Preparation Time: 10 minutes

Cooking Time: 25 minutes

Nutritional information (Per Serving): Calories: 23, Total Fats: 14g, Carbohydrates: 97g, Proteins: 8g,

Ingredients:

- Sweet potatoes
- 1 tbsp of olive oil
- 1 tbsp of thyme
- Salt
- Black pepper to taste
- 1 cup of spinach
- 1 cup of arugula

- 1 tbsp of balsamic vinegar
- 1 cup of whole brie cheese
- 1 cup of tomatoes
- 1 cup of Peppa peppers
- 1 cup of olives
- 1 cup of Cured meats

Directions:

- Turn the oven temperature up to 360 degrees F.
- Arrange the sweet potatoes in an even layer on a baking tray, and then season them with oils, salt, peppers, and a 1/2 teaspoon of thyme. Secondly, place sweet potatoes on a baking sheet and bake in the oven for about 25 to 30 minutes, or until soft.
- The brie cheese should be cut open, the leftover thyme should be added to the top, and then it should be baked with the potatoes.
- Place the brie cheese in the middle of the board and divide the sweet potatoes between the board's two edges.
- Toss the baby spinach and arugula, and balsamic, then divide the mixture evenly across the two halves of the board. Arrange the remaining components in a circular pattern. To be served hot.

6.2 Pancake and Frittata Board

Serving: 6

Preparation Time: 10 minutes

Cooking Time: 36 minutes

Nutritional information (Per Serving): Calories: 13, Total Fats: 24g, Carbohydrates: 17g, Proteins: 82g,

Ingredients:

- Goat Cheese
- Chives Frittata
- 6 eggs
- Salt
- black pepper
- 1 tsp of dried chives
- 1 tsp of parsley
- 1 tbsp of butter

- ½ cup of crumbled cheese

Pancakes:

- 1 ½ cups of plain flour
- 2/3 tsp of salt
- ½ tsp of baking powder
- 1 tbsp of granulated sugar
- 1 egg
- 1 cup of milk
- 1 ½ tsp of vanilla extract
- tbsp of butter

Board

- Maple syrup
- Chocolate spread dip
- Fresh fruits
- Cooked bacon
- pork sausages
- Butter
- Fruit juice

Directions:

- To make a frittata together with cheese and chives, first preheat the oven to 400 degrees Fahrenheit.
- In a suitable bowl, mix together the eggs with the salt, peppers, chives, and parsley.
- Put the ingredients in a cast-iron pan and cook it for approximately five minutes over moderate flame for 2 minutes. Add goat cheese over the surface, then put in the oven for up to ten minutes or wait until the frittata is all way through.
- Pancakes:
- In the meanwhile, make some pancakes.

- After that, put the wheat, water, baking powder, and sugar into a medium dish and mix well.
- Create a hole in the middle of the batter, then add the cream, milk, sugar, and butter, eggs and stir until combined.
- Stir each of the ingredients until you have a smooth batter.
- Finally, bring a pan that isn't stick-resistant up to medium heat, and add one-sixth of the batter to the pan. Preheat the bottom side for approximately two to three minutes without spreading the mixture.
- Afterward when flipping the batter cook for a few minutes for two to three more minutes, or when it is golden brown. Put on a platter, then continue the process to create five additional pancakes.
- Board:
- you should arrange frittata in the middle of the board, and then stack the pancakes around it. Add maple.
- Put the chocolate sauce and the syrup in their own individual dishes and put them close to the frittata.
- Place the remaining ingredients in groups that are the same size all around the board.
- Immediately serve after cooking.

6.3 Loaded Brunch Board

Serving: 6

Preparation Time: 10 minutes

Cooking Time: 0 minutes

Nutritional information (Per Serving): Calories: 11, Total Fats: 22g, Carbohydrates: 11g, Proteins: 42g,

Ingredients:

- Fruit jam (Your Favorite)
- Maple syrup
- Greek yogurt
- Chocolate spread dip
- 6 poached eggs,
- Waffles
- Donuts
- 1 ½ cups of cheddar cheese
- 1 cup of Gruyere cheese
- Cured meats
- Fresh fruits
- 1 ½ cups of mixed nuts

Directions:

- Place the fruit jam, maple syrup and chocolate spreading dip in their own individual dishes. Arrange at various locations on the board.
- Arrange sliced boiled or cooked eggs on a plate, and then place the plate in the middle of the board.
- Place the rest of the ingredients in the same arrangement all over the board, and enjoy.

6.4 Southern Charcuterie Board

Serving: 6

Preparation Time: 10 minutes

Cooking Time: 0 minutes

Nutritional information (Per Serving): Calories: 14, Total Fats: 12g, Carbohydrates: 51g, Proteins: 12g,

Ingredients:

- Fig spread Honey
- 7 oz of the cheddar cheese
- 7 oz of Mimolette wedge
- 4 oz of log goat cheese
- Cured meats
- 1 cup of toasted cashew
- 1 cup of roasted pecans
- ½ cup of olives
- Fresh fruits
- ½ cup of dried apricots
- Flatbread slices
- Crackers
- Chips

Directions:

- Place the fig jam and syrup in their own separate dishes. Place plates in the middle of the board, now arrange items listed into similar groups all around the board. Serve

6.5 Pecan Charcuterie Board

Serving: 6

Preparation Time: 10 minutes

Cooking Time: 3 hours

Nutritional information (Per Serving): Calories: 14, Total Fats: 10g, Carbohydrates: 91g, Proteins: 2g,

Ingredients:

- 8 oz of cheese
- 1 cup of ground pecans
- 1/3 cup of maple syrup
- ½ tsp of salt
- ½ tsp of sage
- cups of roasted pecans
- 9 oz of Swiss cheese
- 6 oz of blue cheese
- 6 oz of cheddar cheese
- Crackers
- bread slices
- Cured meats
- Rosemary sprigs
- Fresh sage leaves

Directions:

- Place all of the cream cheese in a container and mix it well until it is completely incorporated. After covering a loaf pan with baking parchment, place the cheese inside the pan. Use a spoon to mold the cheese into the form of the pan. Place in the refrigerator for at least three hours, or until the consistency is set.

- Take the cream cheese out of the refrigerator, invert it on the board, and then make a crust around it using half of the chopped pecans.

- In a small dish, mix the rest of the ground pecans, the syrup, the salt, and the ground sage until the mixture is well blended. Pour dip on the side of the board opposite the creamy log, then arrange the other contents in a crosshatch pattern from across the board. Eat!

6.6 Fall Charcuterie Board (Birthday edition)

Serving: 6

Preparation Time: 10 minutes

Cooking Time: 0 minutes

Nutritional information (Per Serving): Calories: 4, Total Fats: 15g, Carbohydrates: 8g, Proteins: 17g,

Ingredients:

- 1 cup of artichoke
- 1 cup of pepper spread
- Honey
- 9 oz of blue cheese
- 9 oz of goat cheese
- Cured meats
- Mixed nuts
- 1 cup of dried figs
- 1 cup of cherries
- ½ cup of pomegranate seeds
- Fresh berries
- black olives
- Caperberries
- small persimmons
- 1 sprig of rosemary
- 1 sourdough bread
- Crackers
- Chips

Directions:

- Put the artichoke spread, the pepper spread, as well as the honey in their own individual dishes.
- Place the bowls on opposite ends of the board, then similarly arrange the remaining components all across the surface of the board. Serve

6.7 Cuddle Board

Serving: 6

Preparation Time: 10 minutes

Cooking Time: 0 minutes

Nutritional information (Per Serving): Calories: 43, Total Fats: 23g, Carbohydrates: 38g, Proteins: 87g

Ingredients:

- Water crackers
- 1 sliced baguette
- 9 oz of wedge cranberry cheese
- 1 cup of goat cheese
- Soft-ripened cheese
- Cured meats
- Grain mustard
- Tapenade

- Berry jam

Directions:

- Arrange everything on the board, and have fun with it!

6.8 Keto Charcuterie Board

Serving: 6

Preparation Time: 10 minutes

Cooking Time: 0 minutes

Nutritional information (Per Serving): Calories: 13, Total Fats: 33g, Carbohydrates: 37g, Proteins: 7g

Ingredients:

- Cheeses
- Cured protein
- Fresh Fruits
- Nuts, Mixed
- Vegetables (Your Favorite)
- Ranch dip
- Snacks

Directions:

- Put all of the ingredients on the board and start eating as soon as you can.

6.9 Happy Dessert Board

Serving: 6

Preparation Time: 10 minutes

Cooking Time: 0 minutes

Nutritional information (Per Serving): Calories: 73, Total Fats: 23g, Carbohydrates: 237g, Proteins: 4g

Ingredients:

- Snacks
- Fruits
- Sweets
- Mini marshmallows
- Mini peanut butter cups
- White and dark chocolate cubes
- Pistachios
- Pecans
- Macadamia nuts
- Chocolate sauce

- Fruit dip
- Caramel sauce

Directions:

- In the same manner, assemble all of the components, and then enjoy your meal!

6.10 Dinner Charcuterie Board

Serving: 6

Preparation Time: 10 minutes

Cooking Time: 0 minutes

Nutritional information (Per Serving): Calories: 743, Total Fats: 26g, Carbohydrates: 35g, Proteins: 25g

Ingredients:

- Assorted cured meats
- Assorted salami
- Prosciutto
- Beef jerky
- Mixed vegetables
- Cheeses
- Fruits
- Sauces

- Salads

Directions:

- Arrangement of elements should be the same on board, and then you may enjoy!

Chapter 7: Boards For Sports Days

Create a quick, easy, and nutritious snack board for lunch, supper, or any time of the day by making use of whatever foods you already have on hand in the refrigerator or pantry. The use of a snacking board is an effective model to reimagine items that have been left over from earlier meals or to offer foods that one may not otherwise explore. It is the most efficient way to provide food for people without requiring them to prepare it. When a plentiful and bright snack board is given, everybody's excitement level rises to new heights. It's a veritable feast for the taste buds, with tastes ranging from spicy to sugary and crunchy to mushy. It shouldn't take you more than fifteen and twenty minutes to put up a snacking board similar to this one using things you already possess in your fridge or pantry, which makes it an ideal option for any day during the week.

Berries are an excellent choice for those interested in a somewhat more nutritious option. I'm certain that Summer Fruits and Hibiscus Rose Gin will be well received at this establishment. You really can't go wrong with a picnic spread that includes strawberries, raspberries, blueberries, blackberries, and cranberries; these berries make up the perfect complement. The tartness and sweetness of the strawberries will perfectly complement the flavor of your gin (or tonic), making them the ideal accompaniment to your cocktail. Also, who doesn't appreciate the idea that you can simply add berries to your cocktail? You don't always have to think of blueberries as the healthier alternative when you have the option of drinking them.

When planning the ideal get-together for kids, here are some amusing ideas you may want to consider trying:

- Gin Lolli's – Once the ice cubes are frozen, place them in a cold bag and carry them along to your picnic. Fill icicle trays with sliced strawberries and grenadine and freeze. You should dissolve them in the gin once you've added them.

Did someone mention summertime and pitchers filled with gin cocktails? Prepare ahead of time pitcher jugs filled with your preferred gin drinks, you only need to throw in some ice and fruit, and then you're good to flow, and pour.

Cocktails Served in Teapots If you want to have a tiny bit of a laugh, serve your favorite drink in a teapot. Bring some cups with you, and there it is: a new take on the classic tea but don't worry, we won't tell anybody it's made with gin.

7.1 Patriotic Charcuterie Board

Serving: 6

Preparation Time: 10 minutes

Cooking Time: 0 minutes

Nutritional information (Per Serving): Calories: 33, Total Fats: 136g, Carbohydrates: 75g, Proteins: 15g

Ingredients:

- Fresh fruits
- Water crackers
- Chips
- Choco biscuits
- Salami slices
- Tomatoes
- Gruyere slices or white cheddar

- Red jelly
- Blue jelly

Directions:

- Put some blueberries in a little bowl and put it in the middle of the cutting board.
- Place the rest of the ingredients in an even distribution on the board. Experience!

7.2 Hot Dog Charcuterie

Serving: 6

Preparation Time: 10 minutes

Cooking Time: 8 minutes

Nutritional information (Per Serving): Calories: 134, Total Fats: 46g, Carbohydrates: 35g, Proteins: 67g

Ingredients:

- 11 hot dogs
- 11 hot dog buns
- 1 cup of mixed cheeses (Your Favorite)
- 6 slices of bacon
- ½ cup of coleslaw
- ½ cup of onion
- ½ cup of jalapeno
- ½ cup of relish

- ½ cup of pineapple
- ½ cup of mustard
- ½ cup of ketchup
- ½ cup of mayonnaise

Directions:

- Prepare a grill pan by preparing it over a medium flame. Then, place the hot dogs on the grill and cook them for approximately one to two minutes on each side, or until they are lightly toasted and light brown. Place on a platter and set aside.
- To get a golden-brown color on the buns, toast them for one to two minutes.
- Put a hot dog in each bun, then place them in a row on the board.
- Put the remaining ingredients into their respective bowls one by one, and then arrange them and Serve fresh!

7.3 Gluten-Free Charcuterie Board

Serving: 6

Preparation Time: 10 minutes

Cooking Time: 0 minutes

Nutritional information (Per Serving): Calories: 34, Total Fats: 96g, Carbohydrates: 113g, Proteins: 34g

Ingredients:

- Cured meats, cooked
- Cheese (Any kind)
- Mixed Nuts
- Butter
- Dip sauces
- Fresh fruits
- Dried fruits
- Glute-free snacks
- Pickles veggies
- Asparagus
- Broccoli
- Potatoes

Directions:

- Place all of the components on the board, and then savor!

7.4 Mac and Cheese Charcuterie Board

Serving: 6

Preparation Time: 10 minutes

Cooking Time: 0 minutes

Nutritional information (Per Serving): Calories: 123, Total Fats: 56g, Carbohydrates: 115g, Proteins: 91g

Ingredients:

- 8 oz of dried macaroni
- ¼ cup of heavy cream
- 1 ¼ cups of cheese
- ¼ cup of chopped olives
- ¼ cup of Caper
- ¼ cup of Pickles
- Cured meats

Directions:

- Pasta should be cooked in water that has been gently salted for ten to twelve minutes, or until it reaches the "al dente" texture. After draining the pasta, put it aside.

- In the same saucepan, bring the heavy cream to a simmer over medium heat, and cook for four to six minutes, or until when the volume has been reduced by half. After they have melted, the cheeses should be stirred into the sauce. Add the macaroni, then sprinkle it with salt and pepper, and give it a good toss.

- Put the macaroni and cheese into single-serve dishes and arrange them on the board. Fill the remaining space in the bowls with the remaining ingredients, and serve hot.

7.5 Simple Lunch Charcuterie Board

Serving: 6

Preparation Time: 10 minutes

Cooking Time: 0 minutes

Nutritional information (Per Serving): Calories: 14, Total Fats: 67g, Carbohydrates: 233g, Proteins: 334g

Ingredients:

- 1 large carrot
- 1 bell pepper
- 1 cup of tomatoes
- 1 cup of blueberries
- Dips
- Hummus
- Salmon pate
- Cottage cheese
- ½ cup of walnuts
- 6 eggs,
- Cheese slices (Any Kind)
- Cured meats
- Pita bread
- Wedges Crackers

Directions:

- Place all of the components on the board in their respective groups, and have fun!

7.6 Deli Sandwich Board

Serving: 6

Preparation Time: 10 minutes

Cooking Time: 0 minutes

Nutritional information (Per Serving): Calories: 74, Total Fats: 62g, Carbohydrates: 13g, Proteins: 94g

Ingredients:

- ½-inch thick slices of baguettes
- 1 red onion
- ½ cup of dill pickles
- Dried salami
- Black forest ham slices
- Turkey breasts
- 1 cup of cherry tomatoes
- 1 cup of Parmesan cheese
- 1 cup of white cheddar cheese
- Mayonnaise
- Mustard
- Hot sauce

Directions:

- Baguette slices should be arranged in a circular pattern on a round board.
- The remaining components should be gathered in the middle of the baguette pattern. Enjoy!

7.7 Barbecue Charcuterie Board

Serving: 6

Preparation Time: 10 minutes

Cooking Time: 0 minutes

Nutritional information (Per Serving): Calories: 34, Total Fats: 122g, Carbohydrates: 45g, Proteins: 44g

Ingredients:

- 1 lb. of beef brisket
- 1 lb. of chicken thigh
- cups of sauce, of your choice
- oz of white cheddar slices
- oz of pepper Jack slices
- oz of Colby Jack slices
- ½ cup of cherries
- ½ cup of apricots
- ½ cup of pimento peppers
- ½ cup of pickles
- ¼ cup of jam
- ¼ cup of mustard
- Assorted crackers

Directions:

- Put all of the ingredients on the board in their respective groups, and then serve.

7.8 Mini Individual Charcuterie Board

Serving: 1

Preparation Time: 10 minutes

Cooking Time: 0 minutes

Nutritional information (Per Serving): Calories: 35, Total Fats: 76g, Carbohydrates: 85g, Proteins: 456g

Ingredients:

- ½ cup of cheddar cheese
- 4 slices of blue cheese
- 4 slices of white cheddar
- slices of goat cheese
- Cured meat: prosciutto
- Salami
- Crackers
- Fruit jam
- Hummus

Directions:

- Prepare the dish by arranging all of the components on a small board then present on the board with hummus and jam.

7.9 Plant-Based Charcuterie Board

Serving: 6

Preparation Time: 10 minutes

Cooking Time: 0 minutes

Nutritional information (Per Serving): Calories: 145, Total Fats: 67g, Carbohydrates: 97g, Proteins: 45g

Ingredients:

- 1 ½ cups of celery sticks
- 1 ½ cups of radish slices
- Almond dip
- Cashew chip
- Toasted almonds
- Cashews
- Pecans

- sunflower seeds
- Pumpkin seeds
- Sesame seeds
- Grapes
- Lemon wedges
- Pitted Kalamata olives
- Crackers
- Vegan feta cheese
- Vegan cheddar cheese
- Teriyaki tofu cubes

Directions:

- Put all of the components together, and then dig in!

7.10 Valentine's Day Charcuterie Board

Serving: 2

Preparation Time: 10 minutes

Cooking Time: 0 minutes

Nutritional information (Per Serving): Calories: 65, Total Fats: 97g, Carbohydrates: 787g, Proteins: 57g

Ingredients:

- fresh strawberries
- fresh raspberries
- dried strawberries
- Soft goat cheese
- Baked brie wedge
- White cheddar cheese
- Triple cream cheese

- Cured meats
- Salami
- prosciutto
- Crackers and chips
- Chocolate hearts
- Red valentine
- M & M's
- Sugared almonds
- Candy'sdy hearts
- Honey
- Cashew butter

Directions:

- Arrange all of the components on the board, and then savor the meal with the person you hold most dear.

Chapter 8: Seasonal Charcuterie Boards

Cheese, as well as cured meats, are available throughout the year; however, this does not preclude you from creating a charcuterie board that is packed with items that are in season during a certain event or time of year in order to help you enjoy that holiday or period of the year. Let's see look at different examples of how you may make the ideal charcuterie boards for the spring, summer, autumn, and winter seasons.

8.1 Spring

The arrival of spring is often associated with the beginning of something new, and it is also the time of year when people have a natural tendency to choose lighter, fresher meals over the heartier dishes that are typical of winter menus. Consider incorporating some springtime fruits and vegetables, such as artichokes, strawberries, and radishes, on a charcuterie board for springtime, along with some lighter additions, such as a yogurt dip made with lemon. In addition to that, you could wish to incorporate some fresh goat cheese. If you top the board with a generous number of fresh herbs, you will have a charcuterie board that is suitable for an Easter celebration, a spring picnic, or a dinner party.

8.2 Summer

Since hosting gatherings outside is a signature summer activity, now is the ideal time to provide guests with a charcuterie board that showcases the finest products the current harvest season has to offer. During the summer, there are many fruits and vegetables that are at their peak of freshness and flavor, giving you an abundance of alternatives to choose from. Some of these selections include tomatoes, berries, and other brightly colored fruits and vegetables. For a scrumptious and one-of-a-kind seasonal touch, consider including grilled baguette slices as well as smoked sausage on your board. This is possible given that grilling is a common way of food preparation throughout the summer.

8.3 Fall

The fall is a time of year when we start to seek heavy and rich meals, an autumn charcuterie board should contain meats and cheeses that have a robust flavor profile. Sweetening the dish just a little bit may help balance out the stronger tastes. On a charcuterie board, some items that look and taste great are candied walnuts, fresh figs, and sliced pomegranates, for instance. Think about what additional seasonal touches your guests would love, such as pickled mustard seeds or apple butter, and include them in your preparations.

8.4 Winter

Because preserved meats were traditionally created for the winter season, a charcuterie board is the ideal first dish for a Christmas party or other event that takes place during the winter season. When creating your winter charcuterie boards, don't be afraid to use bold tastes in the meats and cheeses you choose. Choose dried fruits, jellies, and other preserved delights for the other objects on the board, in addition to the usual olives, crackers, and such, as well as classic wintertime delicacies such as oranges and cranberries, if you want to mix things up a little from the standard fare.

8.5 Regional Charcuterie

You might also build a charcuterie board based on a concept, such as a certain area or country, for example. Choose a place that is famous for its meat and cheeses, such as Italy or France, and attempt to include only those meats and cheeses that have been initially created in that region, even if you buy an equal manufactured in the United States. Check to verify that your pick of beverages likewise comes from the nation.

There is no rule that says regional charcuterie boards may only be found in European nations. Choose a certain location to focus on while putting up an American charcuterie board. You should consider Lancaster County as one of your top choices for a location. The place is renowned for producing some of the finest meats and cheeses in the United States, on par with those of Europe.

8.6 Tips For Arranging a Charcuterie Board

It might be argued that the design of your charcuterie board is just as significant as the meats and cheeses that you place on it. By bearing these hints in mind when preparing a charcuterie board, anybody may make it seem aesthetically appealing.

Start with Bowls and Jars

You should begin by putting any dishes or jars on your board that you want to use. This will contain condiments such as olives and pickles, as well as dips, spreads, and jellies. Put some distance between the dishes and jars, and make sure there is enough room between them for the various types of meats, cheeses, and other foods. Include any tools that your guests will have to pick up foods from bowls or spread jams and spreads on bread or crackers.

Space out Meats and Cheese

After you have placed your bowls on the board, the following step is to position your meats and cheeses where you would want them. Instead of placing all of the meats close to one another and all of the cheeses together, spread the meats and cheeses out over the board in an even distribution. Make an effort to alter the look of various types of meat and cheeses so that there is more visual variation. Some cheeses, for instance, are best served in their full wedge form, while others are cut into slices or cubes.

Pops of Colors

Make absolutely sure you have something on hand that can provide a splash of vibrant color to the scene. You will be able to add some visual appeal to your board with the aid of this. It's possible that your charcuterie board may have a somewhat uniform, earthy color palette that's lacking in variation because of the meats and cheeses that you choose for it. This will depend on your selections. A splash of color here or there may make all the difference in this predicament. Tomatoes and strawberries are two examples of foods that may provide a splash of red, while clementines and carrots can add a splash of orange.

Small items to fill Gaps

After the majority of the components of your charcuterie board have been assembled, you can then fill in the spaces with any additional nibbles or fruits and nuts that you choose. Spread the nuts and fruits out over the board rather than grouping them all together on huge charcuterie boards. Instead of grouping all of the nuts and fruits, distribute them on the board. Place a small row and pile it in one location and yet another in a separate one entirely. This contributes to the appearance of a board that is filled with diversity, like a cornucopia, as opposed to a partitioned platter. Cornucopia is a word that comes from the Latin word for "horn of plenty."

Use Herbs

As a finishing touch, add some fresh herbs as a topping to your charcuterie board to give it that extra something special. Herbs such as rosemary, basil, and thyme may provide an extra splash of color, assist you in filling in any barren patches, and give a delightful aroma to enhance the overall sensory experience. Add sprigs of herb to various locations on the board so that they are spread out. To keep cheese slices or bowls from sliding around on the plate, insert a few sprigs below them.

Chapter 9: Charcuterie Trends

The attractiveness of charcuterie will always be strong; nevertheless, the manner in which it is served and the components that are favored will change over time. Surprise your guests by offering them the most recent charcuterie board trends.

9.1 Vegan Charcuterie Board

It's possible that you're curious about how to build a vegan charcuterie board, given that meat and cheese are often the primary components of a classic charcuterie board. You can, thankfully, build a charcuterie board that is totally free of animal products by making a few little alterations. There is an abundance of high-quality vegan cheese alternatives that may serve as a suitable substitute for dairy cheese on the market today. Forego the meats and focus instead on piling your plate high with fruits, chips, and spreads. Include plant-based substitutes for meat, such as roasted chickpeas, bacon made from eggplant, and jerky made from smoked mushrooms.

9.2 Charcuterie Cones

Handheld charcuterie boards are what are known as "charcuterie cones," and they are presented on disposable cones. Among the several types of single-serve charcuterie, charcuterie cones offer the most cost-effective option for companies such as food trucks and other off-site eating establishments. It is more cost-effective to serve charcuterie in disposable paper cones rather than to purchase a large number of little charcuterie boards or use jars.

9.3 Jarcuterie

The term "jarcuterie" refers to a portion of charcuterie that is served in a charming jar or reusable cup in the form of an individual dish. The charcuterie that is served in little mason jars is a popular option. The epidemic was the impetus for the birth of the fad known as "charcuterie in a jar," which has since gained the hearts and bellies of many who like eating charcuterie. Because they are easily transportable and enable guests to nibble while mingling, jarred meats and cheeses are the ideal portable appetizer choice for parties that are catered. In comparison to disposable cones, jars have a more sophisticated appearance.

9.4 Dessert Charcuterie

Even though dessert charcuterie boards aren't actually charcuterie in the traditional sense, they have become a popular method of offering desserts. The display style of a regular charcuterie board is appropriated for the purpose of creating a dessert charcuterie board, which provides customers with a variety of sweet morsels to nibble on. Candied meats are a great alternative for including meats on a dessert charcuterie board if you do wish to include meats. You may also choose to omit the protein and go right for the indulgence if that's more your style. The following are examples of popular additions to a dessert board:

- Hazelnut, chocolate hummus, caramel, and whipped cream are some of the dips that are offered.
- Cheese: mascarpone, whipped mozzarella and honey, cranberry goat's cheese, and whipped ricotta with honey.
- Fresh berries, papaya slices, dried apricots, apple slices, and date slices are all examples of fruit.
- Sweets with a salty bite, such as chocolate-covered pretzels, caramel corn, and candied nuts
- Various forms of chocolate, such as truffles, bark, and nuts coated in chocolate, On a sweet's charcuterie board, cookies—particularly bite-sized cookies with a satisfying crunch—are used in lieu of crackers.
- Candied bacon, burned ends, and hot honey are some of the meat options. Belly of pork with a glaze.

9.5 Charcuterie Skewers

Charcuterie skewers seem to be the ideal thing to have on an appetizer tray for a cocktail party since they allow guests to keep one hand free to hold a wine or cocktail glass. This would also provide your board with the ability to create precise little bits of taste. Choose meats, cheeses, pickled foods, nuts, and fruits that complement each other for each skewer. Guests will likely love numerous products in the same bite.

Conclusion

Don't bother buying pricey flowers and decorations if you're simply going to toss them away or forget that you bought them in the first place!

Investing in a centerpiece that can be eaten will give you a better return on it. It's an achievement because you get to consume it and admire it at the same time.

Charcuterie boards, in addition to being a pleasurable and convivial way to eat, are also the way that humans were designed to eat in the first place. Consuming many smaller meals throughout the day, rather than one huge meal consumed all at once, is easier on the digestive system. Taking the effort to put together a flavor profile that is tailored to your preferences also helps you relish each mouthful. A well-balanced charcuterie board has components that are both sweet and salty, crisp and smooth, and substantial and light. Aside from those two things, you are free to use whatever fruits, meats, cheeses, vegetables, legumes, spreads, or bread you choose.

Because of the range of tastes offered by charcuterie boards, a wide variety of wines may be successfully paired with them. This is another fantastic aspect of these plates. Remember to bring a selection of wine along with you to the social gathering that you are attending if you are bringing it aboard. You may experiment by preparing nibbles that go well with each kind!

Do you remember all those times when you went out and purchased a bunch of food, but nobody ended up eating it? When you have a charcuterie board, though, you won't need to worry about it at all. The mouthwatering presentation will immediately attract guests' attention. This also means that you will spend less time trying to search for boxes and the perfectly matched lid to shop away food scraps, and you also will not be concerned about trying to eat all of the food by yourself before everything spoils because you won't have to worry about attempting to consume all of the food by yourself before it spoils. One cutting board for all of your meals equals just one mess. Even if you have a number of charcuterie boards, you won't have to make a number of trips to collect all of the dishes, nor will you have to battle to figure out how you're going to get all of the oddly shaped dishes into the dishwasher. The mess may be removed with only a single minute spent washing. In the beginning, charcuterie boards were considered to be a sign of great social rank. Charcuterie boards have, and will likely continue to in the future, continue to exude an air of pretentiousness. There is something about presenting food in a way that is not conventional that has the ability to give the impression that an event is nicer than it really is. In addition, you and your guests will have earned the right to experience moments here and there in which you are made to feel as if you are on the edge of the peak.

Most used ingredients

- Curated Meats
- Cheese
- Condiments
- Bread
- Crackers
- Nuts
- Stocking
- Utensils
- Bowls
- Drinks
- Ranch dip
- Cheddar dip
- Honey
- Meats
- fresh fruits
- Dried fruits
- Olives
- Chips
- Almond dip
- Cashew chip
- Toasted almonds
- Pecans
- sunflower seeds
- Pumpkin seeds
- Sesame seeds
- Grapes
- Lemon wedges

- Pitted Kalamata olives
- Crackers
- Vegan feta cheese
- Vegan cheddar cheese
- Teriyaki tofu cubes
- dried macaroni
- heavy cream
- Caper
- Pickles

Made in the USA
Las Vegas, NV
05 December 2023